Flowers from a Horse

Written By:
Jose Arreola

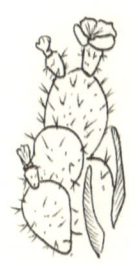

Design & Layout By:
Jorge Ramirez
Jose Arreola

Cover Art & Illustrations By:
Mario Sanchez

Dear Soul,

This is my letter to you:

You deserve peace. You deserve harmony. You deserve to express yourself, in all the ways that you wish to.

You are so pure, so unique, so strong, so brave. You deserve to be free, for the world to witness, for the world to feel and see.

And I hope, that one day soon, serenity comes along and finally finds you.

Love Always,

The Body That Host' You

Petals

home.
stability.
words i don't know.
words i don't see.
words i don't speak.
words i don't keep.
words i don't understand.
they're not a familiar language to me.
they've never been a part of my vocabulary.

chaos.
destruction.
those are the words of "home" to me.
those are my meanings of "stability."

that's all i know.
that's all i've seen.
that's all we've grown to be.

i've tried so hard to be at peace,
but these pieces of me are so broken,
that i can't even find the courage to run,
to leave,
to put these pieces back together
for me.

this darkness.
this sadness.
this pain.
this suffering.

it's slowly taking over everything.

what am i to be?

don't lose your shine little firefly,
it will all be alright.

don't let life put out your light.

in the depths of the darkness,
in the late, late nights,
always remember,
you're made to burn bright.

shinning.

keep

just

-

i must be going *crazy*.

i must be going *out of my mind*.

lately
i just can't seem to find
the *boy* that *i*
had left behind.

it's *innocence* lost.

it's **innocence** gone.

his *innocence*?
my **innocence**?
there's none at all.

can we turn back the time?

give me another try
at this thing called
"*love* and **life**"

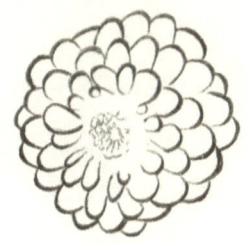

because i'm gone

way ***out of my mind***

and it looks like

i'm afraid

i'll just be going ***crazy***

again

tonight.

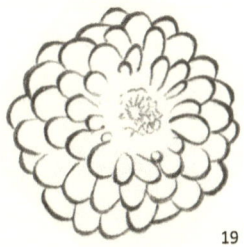

don't feel like myself lately,

arms are heavy,

like something died,

knees are weak.

after it cried itself to death

heart is hurting,

and buried itself

eyes can't see.

deep down inside me lately.

mind is bleeding.

the sun isn't shinning on me lately.

i'm still alive,

darkness is suffocating the life

but i can't breathe.

that's all around me lately.

why is this pain

can't run and hide.

stuck

broken wings can't seem to find

on

a way to fly away

repeat?

lately.

i

go

deep

real deep
inside my mind.

i lose $c_o{}_n{}^t{}_r{}_o{}^l$
$f^r{}_e{}^a{}_k$ $^o{}_ut$ *sometimes.*

but if you just hold me close
and hold me tight,
you can calm my heart,
you can tame my mind.

until then,
i'll be *overthinking*
until sunrise.

those insecurities,
that jealousy.
it runs **deep** in my veins,
it blinds my eyes,

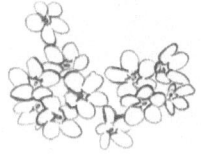 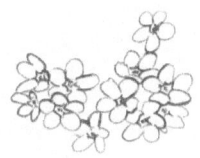

only
sometimes.

i did all of this for *you*.

you.
you.
you.
~~you~~.
YOU.
you.

> *- what in the hell*
> *was i thinking?*

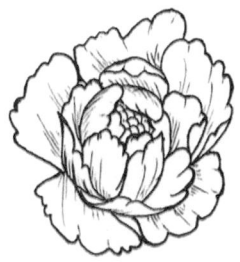

you see,

the problem is,

that i loved you

way more than i loved me.

i put you ***way*** above me,

way before me.

that's definitely where i went wrong,

with everything.

sometimes you over love something *so much*

that it overpowers your entirety.

and that definitely had to stop,

as of yesterday.

i fall
too fast.
i rush,
too quick.

i get all in my head,
it's over
before i know it.

i don't move
too slow,
i just j^{um}p for it.

heart first.

that's why i try to *stay away*
from it.

when it comes to **love,**
well...

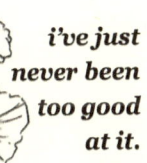 *i've just
never been
too good
at it.*

25

i tried to love you,
but you *B*roke my heart.
i tried to live you,
but you tore me apart.
this was only tempor*A*ry,
i knew that from the start.
never a *"forever and ever"*
it wasn't supposed to last this long.
if you *T*old me to crawl
i'd ask *"how far?"*
i've played such a foolish part.
i tried to leave you,
but i'm addicted *T*o your scars.
you're such a master
at playing your cards.
but i'll be gone soon,
i can final*L*y feel the healing
in what's left of my wounded heart.
so goodbye my darling,
you should know that th*I*s is hard.
but i can no longer be in your bubble,
do what you tell me to,
be your dumb little star.
i've got to cha*N*ge me,
get out of the dark.
find the strength inside me,
break free from your strings and arms,
face the real enemy
and *G*et ready

to put up my permanent guard.

i've been s e a r c h i n g ,

soul searching,

strong searching,

for so long...

when will i reach

my destination?

maybe i wasn't meant to be kept.

maybe i wasn't meant to be tamed.

much like the water,
maybe i was meant to travel.

maybe i was meant to wander.

to be **wild** and *free,*
not captured and sane.

maybe you're not meant to hold to me
to keep.

i slip right through your fingertips,
because out in the open
is where i'm meant to be.

if this is my natural nature,
my "*maybe*" meant meaning,
then i'm happy to say...

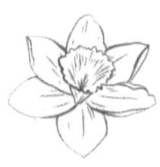

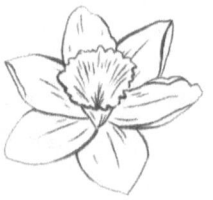

i'm much like the river,

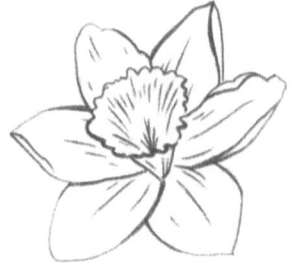

you sea.

i love the broken.

the shattered to pieces.
the **bruised**.
the fucked up

the crazy
the insane

give me those.

they're just my type.
they're just my kind.
they're just my tribe.

the ~~hurt~~.

the ~~heartless~~.

the ~~lost~~.

the ~~stolen~~.

the ~~beaten~~.

the forgotten.

i like to try to fix them.

love them back to life.
put a little *hope* back into their mind.

show them that love is real.
show them that love is kind.
show them that there is love in this fucked up life.

give them all i have to sacrifice.

they're still perfect in my eyes.

and that's how

i only wish

to also be loved.

and *oh how i wish*

you would have only known

how

to love

me

right.

you said i couldn't do it,

so i did it.

you said i wouldn't make it,

so i made it.

you buried me alive

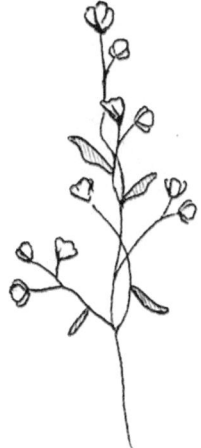

but i'm still breathing.

grounded in this moment.

grounded in this time.

grounded

for all the reasons
that *seem so right*.

grounded.

for **once** in my life.

grounded by the beauty.
by the nature.
by the *want*.
by the w a t e r and sun.

to look so healthy.
to burn so warm.
to shine so ***bright***.
to feel so real.
to feel so alive.

grounded like this,

won't you take me with you?

embrace me fully.

wherever you are.

wherever you stand.

wherever you grow.

to be one with you completely.

to stay grounded
for the rest of my life.

eternally.

eternity.

something i've never known.

something i've never seen.

something to keep me believing.

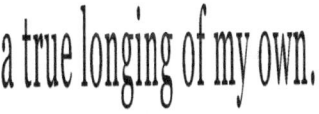
a true longing of my own.

this life

is so fucking crazy.

so am i.

luckily

i'm a pretty little *wreck*.

a pretty little *mess*.

a pretty little **nightmare**.

      and it's always like this.

this is how it always ends.

i sabotage.

i self-destruct.

i push away.

      i fuck it all up.

i destroy.

i run away.

after my hands

are covered

      *in **regret and guts***.

all these roads,
have all of these memories
and they're *trying* to ~~kill me~~.

but i never show up

to the **murder scene**.

they can ***keep*** on calling my name.
they can ***keep*** on aiming at me.

but they will **never** *catch me.*

they will ~~*never*~~ *get to me.*

i am a destination
they can *no longer* reach.

no matter

how $h_a u^n{}_t i^n{}_g{}_l{}_y$

they s p e a k .

their killing spree

will ***keep on*** *missing me.*

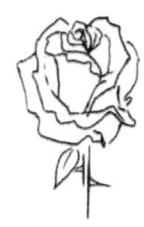

all of these memories

~~will not~~

be the death of me.

yeah,

you knocked me d$_{own}$,

but i'll get back u^p *again*.

- *that's the thing*

about being this

unbreakable

human.

i will **rise**.

i will **conquer**.

with all the **power**
i've **invested** in me,
i will **not** *falter*.

i'm **not** going *down*.
i'm **not** going *under*.

i will **stand**.
i will *fight*.

<u>unlike you,</u>

i was made

to survive.

≡ *Driving Tip:*

the speed limit
is *however* **fast**
you want to go.

if the authority comes

well then

that's when you decide

do you stop,
pull over
and surrender?

or do you keep going

just a little bit

faster?

**THIS LIFE
IS YOUR
ROAD.**

**YOU CHOOSE
THE
ANSWER.**

i have all of this *fire*
burning
inside of me.

it *fuels*
every inch
every part
of my **passionate** *body.*

it's in *every* word.
it's in *every* move.

there's *flames*
in _everything_
that i love
to do.

can't you see?
there's so much gasoline
to ignite
inside of you.

my view from here
is looking pretty **clear**.

tell me,

how's your view looking

from way back there?

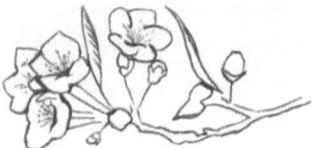

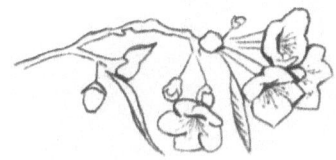

what have i been up to?

well,

i've been living,

how about you?

i get it

you see me as a threat.

that's good.

you should.

why wouldn't you?

don't
    worry,

  i
   got

you.

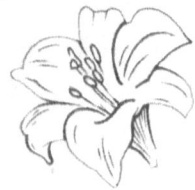

don't you count me ~~out~~.
don't you ~~doubt~~ me now.

i'm not over quite yet.

i'm not finished
place your bets.

~~i'm no joker~~
~~i'm no queen.~~

am i a jack
or am i a king?

don't be a fool.

with tricks up my $sl^{ee^{v^e}}$
you'll see me and w_eep.

go ahead
play this $g^a{}_m b^l e$.

solve the $^r{}_i d^d{}_l e$.

witness me
and you'll see.

the thing about games is...

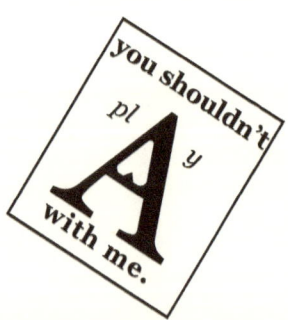

48

i don't follow **you**.

i don't keep up with *you*.

i don't look up to *you*.

i don't worship you.

i don't idolize *you*.

i don't praise *you*.

i don't belong to **you**.

i don't breathe *you*.

i don't see *you*.

i don't dream of you.

i don't think of *you*.

i don't acknowledge *you*.

those are just *some*
of my new rules.

i refuse
to go back
to all things ~~you~~.

and then something happened. i remembered who the hell i am.

where the

FUCK

had i been?

close your eyes.
lift up your chin.

breathe in
breathe out.

(((zone out,
 to zone in.)))

relax a little bit.

center your thoughts.
control your mind.

be still.
be silent.

open your heart.
open your hands.

let out
what you don't want to leave in.

- this is where
you will find
all of your medicine.

i'm financially broken,

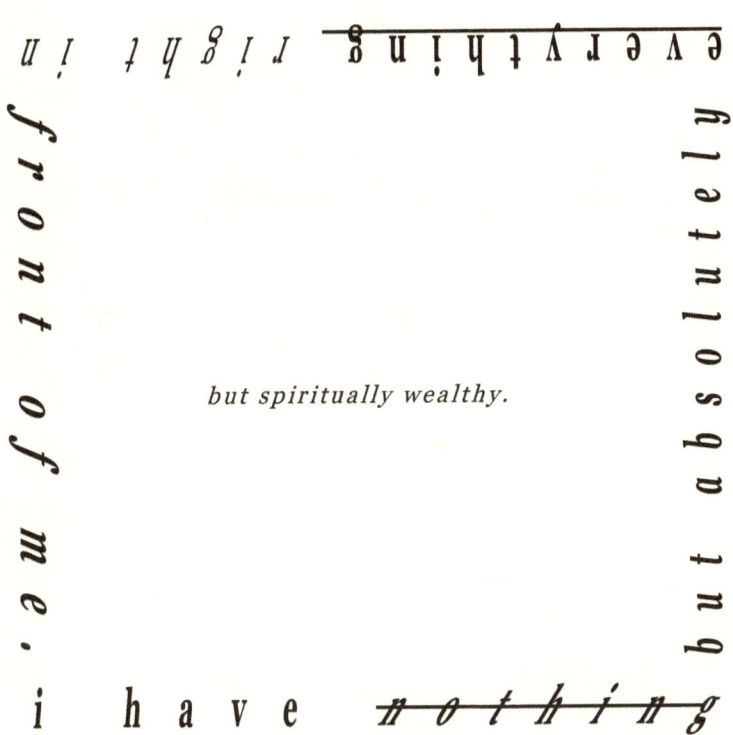

but spiritually wealthy.

i have ~~nothing~~ but absolutely everything right in front of me.

WAKE *UP*

you have
dreams
to make
*a **reality.***

in my world,
there are ~~no boundaries.~~

there is ~~no right,~~
there is ~~no wrong.~~

i a m f r e e t o e x p r e s s m y s e l f
in all the ways
that i wish to.

i create everything.

i welcome it all.

            - *so should you.*

my advice is simple,
LOVE.

love **so much**
that you forget what it's like
to be ***without*** it.

accept all that you are,
all that you have to give.
embrace it.
then give it to the world
to cherish it.

my advice to you
would be
to ***love to death***.

dream of rainbows.

because that darkness,

it will lock you up.

it **will**

keep you

forever c_old.

let that light in.

give it a chance...

there is so much m o r e

that love

has

to give.

it's a **shame**.

all you have to offer the world is your beauty and not your

b r a i n .

you better learn how to love that skin that you're in.

it's all that you've got,
even after this life ends.

there is no, *"for rent"*
there is no selling, returning or even exchanging.
you don't get a receipt for that,
not even a second chance.

i hope you make that skin that you're in
a beautiful and comfortable living,

all while this lasts.

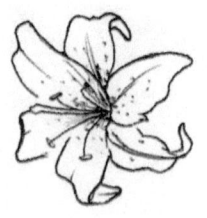

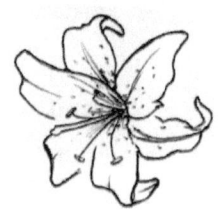

even if you can be a unicorn,
always be yourself.
you already are *magical,*
powerful,
unique and *rare,*
just as you are.

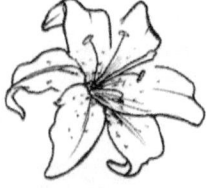

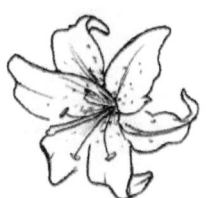

there is no need

to want to be

anything more ***mystical***.

BE YOU

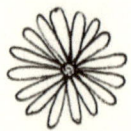

that's the most fearless thing
that you can ever do.

you have ***the right***.

the *right*

to right

your

    pretty

        little

   f u c k e d u p

  heart out

baby.

right it out
w i s e l y.

at some point

you ~~stop~~ *c a r i n g .*
    just

who comes.

who g o e s .

who **stays**.

because the truth is,

that at some point,

every person you love,

in some type of way,

is *going* to br e a k your heart.

just as *you*
will break their hearts as well.

and *somehow,*

in *some* type of way,

that's all okay.

FORGIVE.

no matter what they've done to you,
how they've wronged you.

no matter how much it hurts,
how much it pains you.

you must always forgive.

fore if you don't,
you won't be able to *truly peacefully live.*

you won't be able to *truly let that light in.*

in order to let go,
<u>you have to forgive.</u>

today is a brand new day.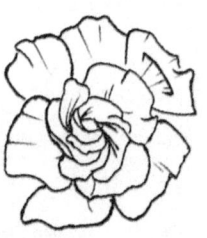

and with brand new days,

come brand new

beginnings.

my *time* is coming,

my *time* is <u>now</u>.

there's ~~no time~~ for hurting,

~~no time~~ to stay on the ground.

if i can just keep r i s i n g,

my *passion* will scream so loud.

26 years

and i still have fears,

but i'm facing them all on my own.

26 years

and i've cried many tears.

broken some hearts,

even my own.

26 years

and i'm still standing here.

choices i've made.

memories i've saved.

lessons i've learned.

life can be

so warm and cold,

but you'll be alright,

just keep up the fight.

26 years

and i'm still breathing air.

living proudly

in the way i've made me,

in my soul

and in my bones.

26 years,

my golden year.

and i can feel
that it's my time.
now will i fail
or will i fly?
either way,
i've made it.
i've survived.
i'm alive.

cheers,
to 26 years.

...and you,

you're *so damn* beautiful.

if you only knew

all the ways
that i want to worship your thoughts
and fall
so
deep into your mind.

are.

unawarely

unapologetically,

that you so

the beautiful human

the e$_m$o^{t}i$_o$n^{a}l,

the **physical,**

the mental,

for the **real**,

let me love you.

you can take my pride,
you can take my life,
you can take my tears,
you can take my fears,
but you ~~can't~~ take my heart.

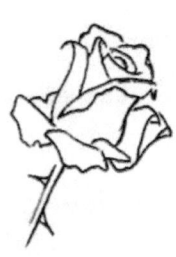

i've worked **too hard**,
i've come ***too far***.
just to give it ^{up}?
you can have **_everything_** you want,
but you will ~~*never ever*~~ have **enough**
to take away
all of my love.

KEEP *GIVING* LOVE.

that's what we all need.

that's what the universe

is *seeking*.

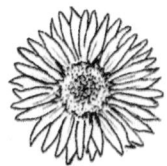

do good.

intentions

be good.

*i **could** do this.*

*this **could** be me.*

but if i did that,

<u>then i wouldn't be living</u>

a u t h e n t i c a l l y .

i'd rather be real,
than be fake.

i'd rather be true,
than be false.

i'd rather be honest,
than be inauthentic.

there is ~~nothing~~ good
that ~~ever~~ comes
from being
~~anything~~
~~but~~ your
~~bare~~
self.

read that again.

loving me *isn't* easy.

it takes a lot of **guts**
to get to my glory.

loving me is cheap,
it will only cost you ***everything***
but your ~~money~~.

loving me consist of time, space and energy.

your patience <u>must</u> be key.
*there **has to be** a sense of peace.*

it takes a lot of understanding.
an open mind
with a heart full of bravery.
to handle,
to tame,
to care for
someone as **bold**,
yet someone as delicate,
as me.

loving me,
is ***everything***,
but *easy.*

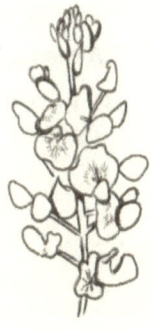

you are going to be *highly*
disappointed in this life,

if you *think* for *once second*,

that someone will do for **you**

as **you** would do for them.

it just *doesn't* work like that.

**(that's just the brutal truth about people,
we can all be very selfish humans.)**

now is ~~not~~ the time

to

f ^{a} ^{l} ^{l} *a* ^{p} *a* ^{r} $_t$.

<u>*now*</u> *is the time*

to

RESTART.

i've taken

all the right

~~and all the wrong~~

chances

and i'm still believing.

we all have our battles.

we all have our scars.

we have all been

through *different* storms.

better days

come and go

but if you *dream*

and you have *hope*

you will see

that you can do

anything

and you will **shine**

brighter than a rainbow.

if you show the world

that *you're unstoppable,*

you're unafraid.

look in side

your *heart* and *soul*

and grab *everything.*

everything that you are,

be it,

embrace it,

love it.

be confident.

~~don't~~ *doubt* yourself.

and you will see

that *anything*

is possible.

and there is **~~nothing~~**

that can **ever,**

ever

break **you.**

now are we afraid of love, //

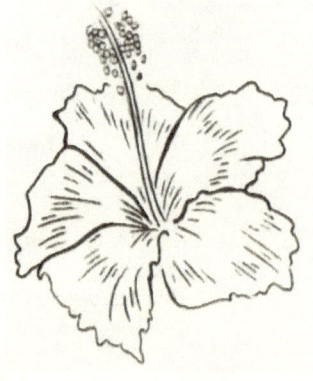

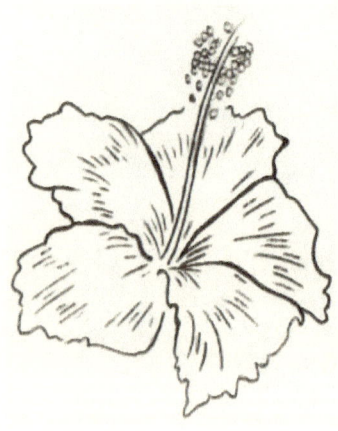

// *or is love afraid of us?*

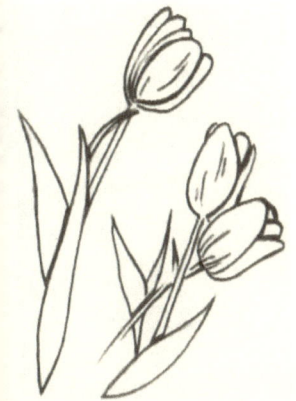

in the end

we've all just managed

to start all these conversations,

by *talking*

to beautiful strangers.

you're gonna want to hold on to me. i'm going places. you'll see...

...i promise you i am worth keeping.

when i get to where i'm going,
i'll leave this all behind.

when i get to where i'm going,
it'll just be me,
myself,
my dreams,
and i.

when i get to where i'm going,
i'll leave you high and
                        dry.

when i get to where i'm going,
it'll be
    the best
            bittersweet

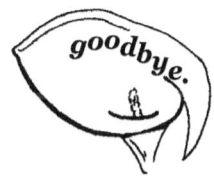

i just wanna *r u n ,*
r u n into the sun.

come with me
and *y o u 'l l s e e ,*
that we are meant to be.

and i know,
i'll never let you go.

you are home.

you make me whole.

please,

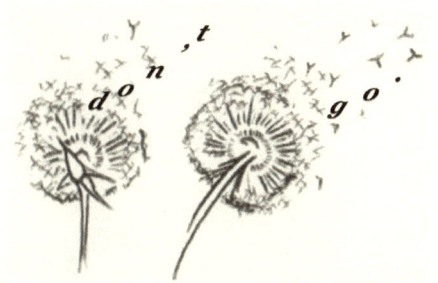

though it may seem that it is over,

does not necessarily mean that it is the end.

my
y
my   life
s
a
n
c
t
u
a
r
y

my *flowers*
are still blooming,
they'll eventually *all*
come to life. when they do,
~~don't you dare pick them.~~
fore *if* you do, i will *slowly die.*

my petals may be falling, **<u>but</u>** *much like the cycle of life,*
when one ~~dies~~, another one is coming, to keep me *alive.*

it's a tempting
touch, a tempting
smell, even a tempt-
ing bite.
all of my daises, my
roses, my tulips are
the beautifulest *sight.*

but love me from
afar. i blossom *best,*
when i'm ~~*not*~~ in
your arms.

you can *water* my
roots and give me
sunlight, but to
keep me
is ~~forbidden~~.
my soil is *best*
when it's left
right.

and that is how
my garden goes,
this is how my
garden...

grows.

Thank you

The fact that i'm actually doing this right now is so beyond amazing and crazy to me. i always knew i wanted to write, ever since i was 12, i just never thought i'd actually bring any of my real dreams and passions to life. it's amazing what you can do when you dream big and just go for it.

To every single person that followed me on this amazing journey, that supported me, that was just there for me in general, my closest friends and my family (you know who you are), i love y'all so much and i thank you from the bottom of my most humbled heart. this was such a crazy and wild ride for me but it really was the most beautifulest and most spiritual thing i have ever done and have ever given to this earth. i could not have done it without all of the endless love from everyone, thank y'all so, so much. it truly means the world to me and more!

Jorge, i have to give you the biggest THANK YOU i can possibly give and the most love with this, because you are such a genius and i would not have been able to pull this off and put all of this together if it wasn't for you. i love you so much, i hope you know that. i am so lucky and so thankful to call you and have you as one of my best friends. WE DID IT!

Mario, you're awesome and a true artist and a true talent. getting to work with you on this was a dream come true and i look forward to working with you again! you made the horse exactly how i wanted it and i couldn't have asked for a better person to do that for me.

Thank you guys, thank you everyone! i love y'all!

The meaning of this book and the title is simple, to me, in my mind. the horse represents me and the flowers represent everything that fills me. my different emotions, my many, many feelings and my different perspectives on life. the word play and the art that came from that was something jorge and i didn't intend to do, it kinda just unfolded and happened as we were making the book and i'm so glad it did because now it's a work of art all on its own, it's not just a poetry book with words. it intrigues you and plays with your mind and i absolutely love that we made that and made this whole thing come to life.

I just wanted this book to be about me, internally and about how i've handlded and delt with life so far. learning how to love yourself and motivate yourself in some of your most darkest, scariest and saddest times is a very hard thing to pull off and do, but i'm not a quitter and thankfully i still had the people i had there to keep pushing me and telling me to keep going, i will never be able to repay that and they will never know how much that means to me and how close i will forever hold that to my heart. i did this book completely for me, to help shine a little light and inspire the world. i hope it did just that.

I feel horses are my true spirit animal and i just love everything they stand for and what they mean. they truly symbolize everything i admire and cherish. they are such crazy beings but are really just beautiful and completely harmless when you realize that they are sad creatures that just want to run wild, be careless and love freely.

Thank you life, for all of this. i can't wait to see what comes next...

Best,

Jose Arreola